Breathing

By Paul Bennett

Belitha Press

First published in Great Britain in 1997 by

 Belitha Press Limited
London House, Great Eastern Wharf
Parkgate Road, London SW11 4NQ

Editor: Veronica Ross
Series designer: Hayley Cove
Photographer: Claire Paxton
Illustrator: Cilla Eurich
Picture researcher: Diana Morris
Consultants: Jo Ormisher/Elizabeth Atkinson

ISBN 1 85561 595 9

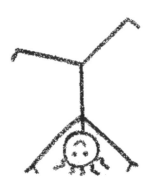

Printed in Hong Kong

Photo credits
Bubbles: 9t Ian West. NASA: 22. Science Photo
Library: 13t Alfred Pasiekia; 15c CNRI; 25t
Eye of Science. Still Pictures: 24 Thomas
Raupach. Zefa: 23b.

Thanks to models Topel, Jodie, Ricky,
Bianca, Meera.

Words in **bold** are explained in the list of
useful words on pages 30 and 31.

Contents

Why do I need to breathe?

You need to breathe to stay alive.

You breathe all the time without thinking about it.

You breathe when you are asleep, and when you brush your teeth.

When you breathe, air is sucked into your **lungs**. A **gas** called oxygen is in the air. Without oxygen, you would die.

The oxygen is used by your body to make **energy**. You need energy when you play sports, read a book or paint a picture, and for everything else you do.

Breathing in

You breathe in through your nose or mouth. Air goes down your throat in a tube called your windpipe.

Inside your chest, the windpipe splits into two tubes which take the air into your lungs.

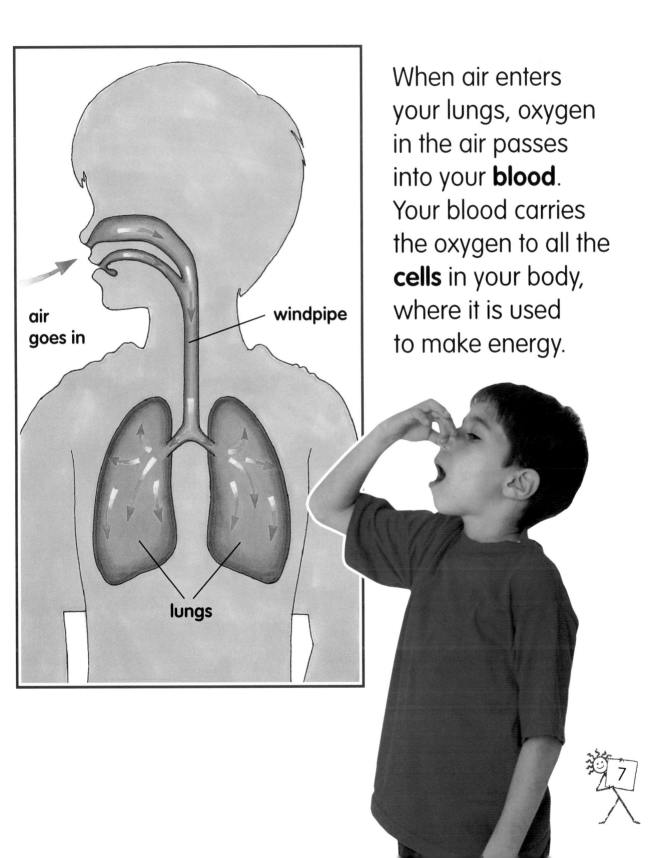

air goes in

windpipe

lungs

When air enters your lungs, oxygen in the air passes into your **blood**. Your blood carries the oxygen to all the **cells** in your body, where it is used to make energy.

Breathing out

When you breathe out, **stale air** is squeezed out of your lungs, up your windpipe and out of your nose or mouth.

air
goes out

windpipe

lungs

8

Stale air has water in it. Breathe out deeply on a cold day. Can you see the water droplets?

A gas called carbon dioxide is in stale air too. The water and carbon dioxide leave your body when you breathe out.

You can blow out about two litres of air in one go. That's enough to fill a balloon.

Your chest

Your lungs are inside your chest. They are protected by the **bones** that make up your **rib cage**.

Stand in front of a mirror and take a deep breath. Your chest becomes bigger.

At the same time, your **diaphragm** moves down. There is now more space for your lungs to **expand** and air rushes in to fill them.

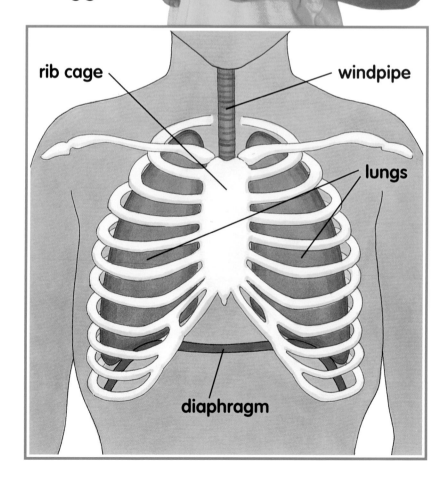

rib cage

windpipe

lungs

diaphragm

When you breathe out, your chest becomes smaller, and your diaphragm relaxes and moves up.

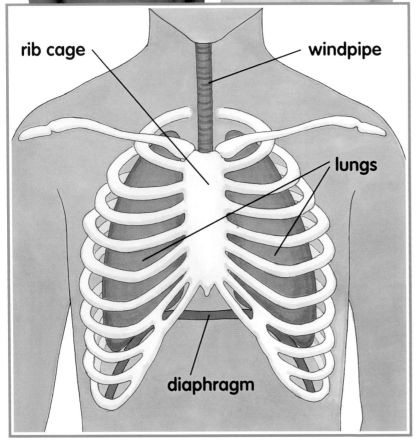

rib cage

windpipe

lungs

diaphragm

There is now less space inside your chest. Stale air is squeezed up and out of your body.

Inside your lungs

Your lungs are like large sponges, but they hold air, and not water.

Inside your lungs, the air passes into lots of tiny tubes, which take the oxygen into your **bloodstream**.

The air tubes in your lungs split into smaller and smaller tubes, like the branches on a tree.

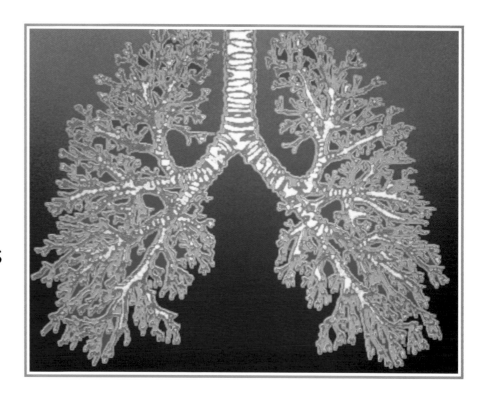

The smallest tubes end in tiny air sacs, like the ones shown here. The air sacs are covered in very tiny tubes called capillaries.

Oxygen from the air sacs passes through your capillaries and goes into your blood.

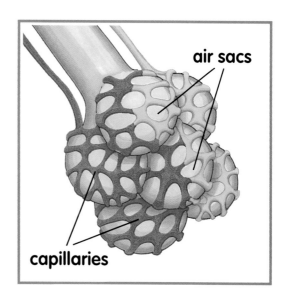

air sacs

capillaries

Your blood

Blood is a liquid that carries oxygen from your lungs all around your body. The oxygen is carried in millions of cells called red blood cells.

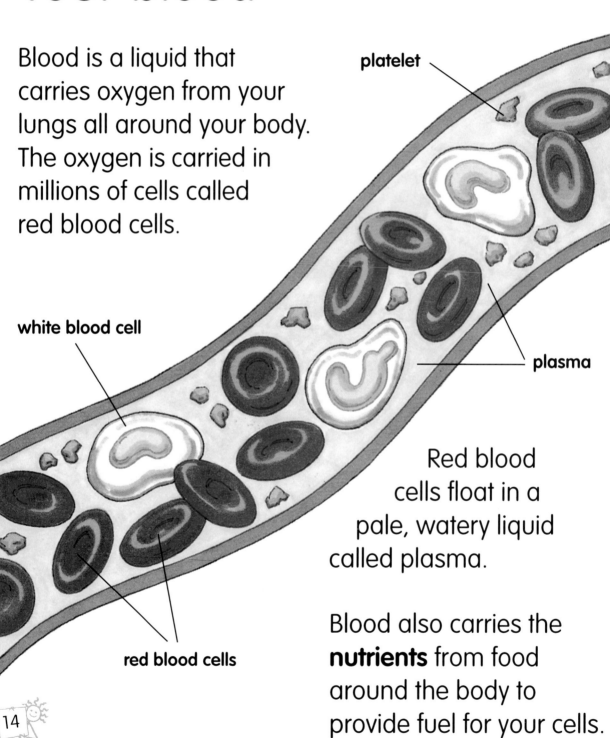

platelet

white blood cell

plasma

red blood cells

Red blood cells float in a pale, watery liquid called plasma.

Blood also carries the **nutrients** from food around the body to provide fuel for your cells.

There are other cells in your blood. White blood cells, like the one shown here, attack germs that enter your body.

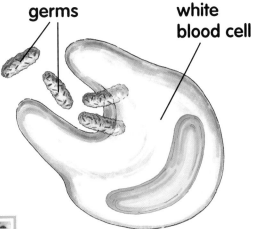

germs

white blood cell

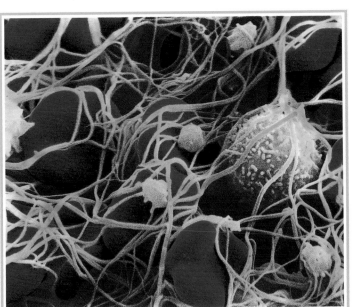

This is a photograph of a blood **clot** taken through a **microscope**. Cells called platelets help your blood to clot and form a **scab** when you cut yourself.

A seven-year-old contains about three litres of blood.

15

What is your heart like?

Your heart is a **muscle** about the size of your fist. It works like a powerful pump, sending blood to all parts of your body.

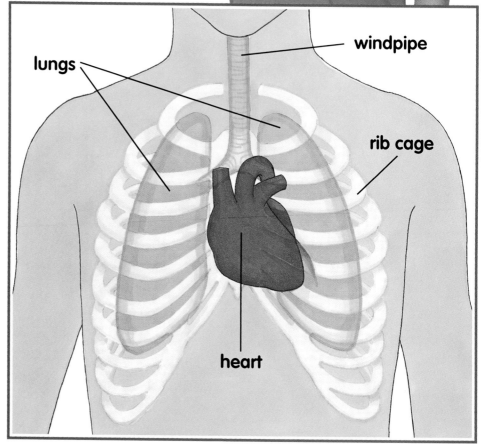

windpipe

lungs

rib cage

heart

Your heart never stops beating. Every time it beats, it pumps blood around your body.

You can feel your heart beating when you exercise.

If you put your ear on your friend's chest, you can hear her heart beating.

A seven-year-old child's heart beats about 80–100 times a minute.

17

Your veins and arteries

Blood is pumped from your heart and carried around your body in tubes called blood vessels.

The blood vessels that carry blood away from your heart are called arteries.

Each artery branches into smaller and smaller tubes. They lead into a network of capillaries.

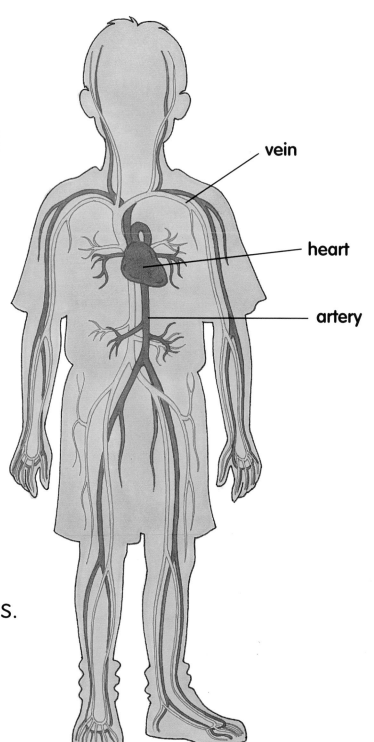

vein

heart

artery

Veins carry the blood
back to your heart,
which pumps it to
your lungs
and back.

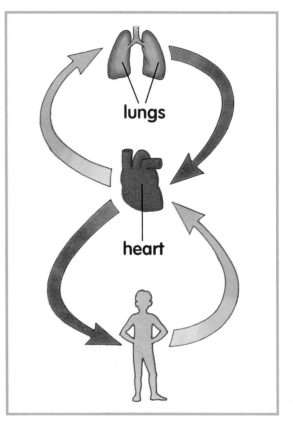

lungs

heart

In this way blood
flows round and
round your body.
This is called
circulation.

You can see your
veins on the back
of your hands.

Out of breath

When you are sitting still, you only need to breathe about 15 times a minute. Count the number of times you breathe in and out in a minute.

When you are resting, you do not need so much energy, so you breathe more slowly and your heart beats slower.

Try exercising hard for a few minutes. How many times a minute do you breathe now?

When you exercise, you need to take in lots more air, so you breathe faster.

Your heart beats faster too, to carry the extra oxygen you need all round your body.

21

The air around you

Air is all around you. It is made up mainly of two gases, oxygen and nitrogen.

The higher up you go, the less oxygen there is in the air.

If you travelled high up into the sky in a hot-air balloon, you would need a supply of oxygen to help you to breathe normally.

There is no air in space, so astronauts must wear a special suit that has its own air supply.

You cannot breathe under water so you must hold your breath.

Divers wear air tanks to help them breathe under water.

Breathing problems

The air around us is made dirty by smoke from factories, cars and lorries. **Polluted air** can damage your lungs and cause breathing problems.

People who smoke often have a bad cough and find it difficult to breathe. Lung and heart diseases can be caused by smoking.

Pollen and dust mites can also cause breathing problems. This is a picture of a dust mite seen under a microscope.

A common breathing problem is asthma. People with asthma can use an inhaler. This puffs out a special medicine that helps to keep the tubes in the lungs open.

Mouths and noses

Your nose is full of hairs that trap any dust or dirt that goes up your nose. Any tiny specks that reach your air tubes are gently swept away from your lungs by tiny hairs.

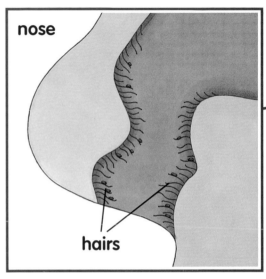

nose

hairs

A sneeze or cough clears your nose or throat and blows dust and pollen out.

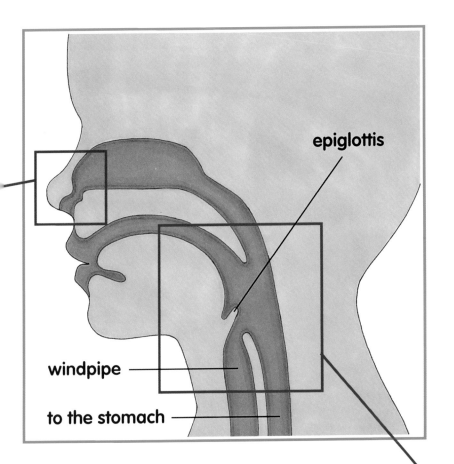

epiglottis

windpipe

to the stomach

If you are in a hurry and swallow food too fast, it may go down the wrong way. When this happens, a cough blows the food out.

The tube that your food goes down is behind your windpipe. When you swallow, a flap called the epiglottis closes over the entrance to the windpipe.

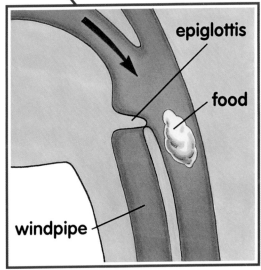

epiglottis

food

windpipe

Making sounds

The air you breathe out is used for talking. Air travels up your windpipe and through your **voice box** to make sounds.

Sounds are made into words by your mouth. Look in a mirror and see how you use your lips, tongue, teeth and cheeks to make words.

Hiccups are caused when your diaphragm suddenly tightens and you take in short, sudden gasps of air.

When you laugh, you let out air in a quick series of short breaths. You sigh with a long breath out and yawn with a deep breath in.

Useful words

Blood
The red liquid that is pumped around your body by your heart.

Bloodstream
The flow of blood around your body.

Bones
The strong and hard parts inside your body.

Cells
Tiny parts that make up your body.

Clot
A thick lump of blood.

Diaphragm
A thin sheet of muscle under the lungs that tightens and relaxes as you breathe in and out.

Energy
What you need to be able to play and work without feeling tired.

Expand
To become larger.

Gas
Something that is like air, not solid and not liquid. Oxygen and nitrogen are two of the gases that make up air.

Lungs
The spongy areas in your chest that you use when breathing.

Microscope
An instrument which you use to look at things closely.

Muscle

A soft, stretchy part inside your body that makes you move. In your heart, the muscle draws together and stretches out, causing your heart to beat.

Nutrients

The useful parts of food that your body needs to stay healthy

Pollen

A fine dust found in flowers.

Polluted air

Air that is made dirty by the dangerous gases pumped out by factories and motor cars. It can damage people's lungs.

Rib cage

The bones in your chest that protect your heart and lungs.

Scab

The hard crust that forms over a cut or graze.

Stale air

Air that you breathe out.

Voice box

The part of your windpipe which makes sounds so that you can talk.

Index